CW01238720

The Last Pair of Ears

Mary F McDonough

To: The DIVINE
Mizz Macpherson:
thanks & much
love

GADFLY

Mary McDonough

First edition published 9 January 2014
by Gadfly Editions

© 2011 Mary F McDonough

British library Cataloguing in Publication Data
A CIP catalogue record for this book is
available from the British Library

ISBN 978-0-9928060-0-2 eBook
ISBN 978-0-9928060-1-9 Hardback
ISBN 978-0-9928060-2-6 Paperback

A limited edition with pigment printed
art is available direct from the publisher

Cover design and artwork
© 2014 Martyn Clark

Designed and typeset in
Adobe Garamond Pro 9 / 11
by Martyn Clark

Mary F McDonough has asserted her right to be identified as the
Author of the work in accordance with the Copyright, Designs and
Patents Act 1988. All rights reserved. No part of this publication may be
reproduced without prior permission. For permission, please contact
Gadfly Editions or the author directly

www.gadflyeditions.com
www.maryfmcdonough.com

I listen, I hear:
I'm the last
pair of ears,
and sometimes
that's enough.

ACKNOWLEDGEMENTS

Thanks to Brendan and Tristan McDonough-Clark for helping with fundraising, Bryony Stocker and Stew Melville for their proofreading support, and Ornan Rotem and Num Stibbe at Sylph Editions for their advice and feedback. Thanks also to David Kinloch for his supervision while I hatched this collection during my M.Res in Creative Writing at the University of Strathclyde.

Many poems in this collection have previously been published elsewhere. *Purple* appeared in *Keith Wright Memorial Pamphlet*, Feb 2011, *Apple Snow* was published as a poster for *Strathclyde Research Day*, Apr 2011, *Spawn* was in *Keith Wright Memorial Pamphlet*, Feb 2012, *Making the Bed* and *Leg Shaving* in *Octavius*, Jun 2012, *My Old Bag* in *Causeway / Cabshair* Dec 2012, *Parasite* in *Valve 3*, Nov 2013, *Nativity* and *Sated* in *Ecloga: Journal of Literature and the Arts,* 2014, and *Apple Snow* in *Flux,* 2014

Excerpts from *Small Stories, Spawn, Shaving & Other Lies, Hopscotch, Clock,* and *We Swim Out* also featured in an improvised album by Martyn Clark, *Hopscotch Requiem*, available to download at www.martynclark.com

The production of this book was supported by generous contributions from many friends, family, and even some kind people we've not yet met. Thank you.

PERSONAL NOTE

The Last Pair of Ears is a collection of poems and short stories about seeing and hearing what we aren't supposed to notice. The two interlocking sets of poetry and short stories represent my exploration of the power of narrative to heal as well as to distort and influence. All of the stories, even those about my own life, have been influenced by my understanding of what it means to be a therapist.

The focus of this collection is on 'lost stories' that have been overlooked, suppressed, or forgotten. In large part, these stories reflect aspects of, and are consistent with 'female' experience. Such stories tend to be marked by flux and loss.

@maryfmcdonough

CONTENTS

LOSS
    Small Stories   10
    Bullet Train to Bedtime   11
    Games   13
    Leg-shaving and Other Lies   15
    Peter's Lost   17
    Spawn   18
    Away Back   19
    Front Lines   20

CARRYING / CARING
    Cupped   22
    Brothers are a Big Responsibility   23
    Close the Window, Open Your Mind   25
    Blue   27
    My Old Bag   29
    Even Bumblebees Stop Buzzing Eventually   31

WOMAN'S WORK
    Dead Leg Dreaming   34
    Apple Snow   35
    Sated   37
    Seasonin'   39
    You Are Such a Wee Darling   41
    Gospel   42

OUT OF MEMORY

Nativity	44
Killing with Kindness and a Compliment	45
Riding the Dementia Express	47
Purple	49
Bye Bye Baby	50
Still Ticking	51
Webbed	52
Family Secrets	53
Clock	54

LOVE IS

Making the Bed	56
Opposite Of	57
Compass	58
Not Here	59
Allies and Enemies	61
Parasite	63
Wave the White Dishtowel	64
The Damn Thing Won't Fit	65
Patience	66

ENDINGS

Last	68
Sacking the Old Bag	69
Battery Grannies	71
Lordy, Hallelujah, and Brownkaydis	75
More Broken	76
Today There Are No More Hallelujahs	77
We Swim Out	78

Loss

SMALL STORIES

The stories are too big to lose, to ignore,
too small for you to notice.

They sit, here and there, dotted
around the landscape, fading from memory.

BULLET TRAIN TO BEDTIME

I waddle back and forth, dragging bags of clothes behind me into the kitchen. A winter's worth of attic dust is in these clothes. Dirt is the enemy, as far as late-pregnancy nesting is concerned.

I wanna wear dem. I doin' dat, Mama. With his brows scrunched together, two angry caterpillars, and his pink, raisin lips, he looks like me. He usually looks like his Dad; I wonder why it is only in anger that he resembles me.

"I know you do, honey, but you are getting too big. The Shinkansen 'jamas don't fit you any more. I'll put them away for your baby to wear some day."

'Jamas say 2 year boy. I 1. His logic is unassailable. He is threatening me with the Negotiator Finger. *I not yike-a dat baby wear my 'jamas. I take train 'jamas out that bag. Now.*

"You are almost two. You have lots of other 'jamas. These are going to be too tight, honey."

He waves Totoro at me. Totoro is suddenly an authority figure, as is the man he has never met, who gave us Totoro and sent Shinkansen pajamas when Brendan was born.

The other pajamas don't have smiling Shinkansen on them. I wonder if outgrowing the bullet trains means growing up. Being too big for these 'jamas might mean that Brendan is too big to be my baby. He is 1 and three-quarters; the track from Shinkansen to adulthood to death seems suddenly short to me. My son is on a trajectory over which I have no control. I can't protect him from mortality.

One 'yast' night is worth doing another load of laundry. I silently wedge him in to the dusty 'jamas, and the Shinkansen smile.

Brendan is heavy in my lap, what is left of it, abruptly asleep. We waddle together to his new big boy bed, in which he, Totoro, and the bullet trains look very small.

GAMES

Hopscotch,
cops and robbers,
ring around the rosies.

Dodge ball,
hide and seek,
among the dusty bluebells.

Games I forgot,
and people too:
now I'm old—
and so are you.

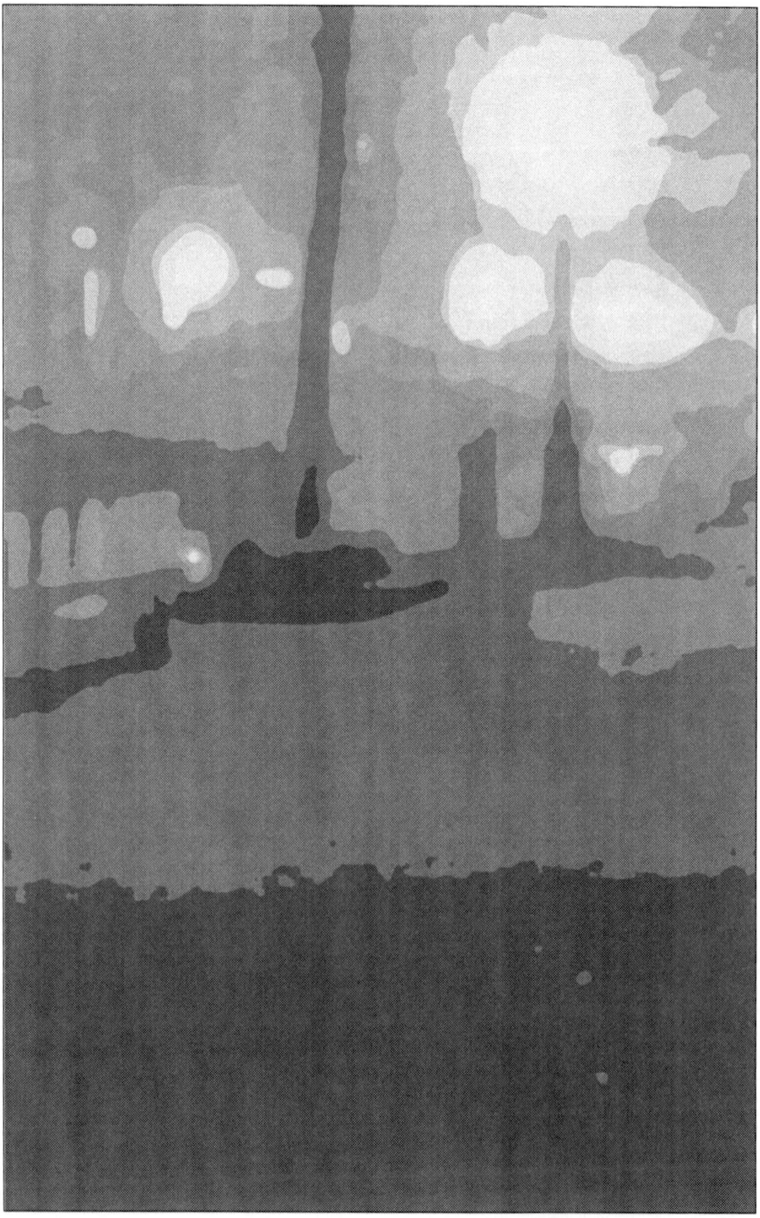

LEG-SHAVING AND OTHER LIES

For a year,
I begged my mother
to let me shave my legs.

"Everyone else is doing it."

"You promised!"

"I'll be careful."

All lies.
More followed:
I didn't tip over the edge of the tub
and into womanhood.

I was still twelve.

Blood ribboned
down my shin
as my brothers laughed.

At recess the next day,
I waited with the rest
against the bricks.

'Choose me, me!' I wanted to shout, but didn't.
Not how the game was played.
My stomach traded places
with my pulse
as he walked over.

He saw the cut, and
left me, standing,
unpicked,
tart with my disappointment.

PETER'S LOST

When's he coming to take me home?
Can you see Peter?
Is Peter in the area?

There's no real food here. It's all
shite.
Ya cannae make me eat this. Or
that.
Where is he?

I am desperate for a piddle.
I need to wee right now!
I'm not a wee girl, but
I'm crying.
I'm not wee!
Why am I crying here?

Where is Peter?
Peter,
are you in the area?
Speak to me, Peter?

Where is Peter just now?
Is Peter here?
Is Peter in the area?

I'll have to die.
I'll just have to die.
Can anyone hear me?

SPAWN

You flop, breathless, gills gaping,
hatched
in a too-temporary desert puddle.

Frogs should know better.
I scoop you up,
and carry you inside,
sloshing,
unseen by adult eyes,
to the glass box
full of grass clippings and rocks.

I put my mouth against my side of the pane,
pressed open,
waiting.

AWAY BACK

Back then, we didn't even go see no doctor 'til we'd missed 3 periods.

No point.

They'da sent us away, if we'd tried any sooner. Wasn't nothin' no family doctor, let alone a specialist, coulda done if we was going to lose a baby.

Nothin' could keep one inside, not onct it decided t' leave.

I never even thought of 'em as babies, just maybes, leastaways not until I felt them kickin'. Any baby made it that far was bound to stay, though sometimes they was borned dead. I don't remember ever feelin' afraid that I would lose one.

So different now, so hard I think.

Women seem to know babies, to feel them, way before they should. Seeing heartbeats on computers, hearin' them, having pictures, all just makes babies real before they should be.

Y'all all show me them pictures, and I cain't never tell one end from the other, and I damn sure don't want to get that wrong, y'all take it sa hard. Head? Butt? Boy? Girl? Babies are better off bein' secrets, secrets women are better off keepin'.

FRONT LINES

Hunched over their maps, two generals plan campaigns. They arrange their armies. The rug is ruched and wrinkled with great care. The terrain is mountainous, populated with goats and flowers.

The generals agree, after 4 arguments and rolling the dice, whose team is The Goodies: silent men, uniformly grey, standing in long, grim, lines. The Goodies fight with honor. The Baddies hide under covers, furniture, behind the door. Virulent, poisonous, they have no scruples.

Wings flap. Bodies flail. Planes fall from the sky. Snakes hiss. Men scream.

The Baddies, ably led by Medusa, several Decepticons, and Polyphemus, defeat the modern warriors who bomb them from stealth planes. Even the snipers, belatedly adopting enemy tactics and hiding in the folds of the rug, are found and eaten.

Next time, shrieks General 1, stomping off, *I'm being The Baddies!*

Carrying / Caring

CUPPED

I am at the sink.
Life continues, a worn track:
I am intent on the ordinary, and on you.

Separating yellow
from white,
teasing strands from the cup of the shell,
I cradle the yolk.
The yolk is what matters.

Its eggy smallness could slip between my fingers,
down a drain,
No matter how careful I am.

Anything could jostle you loose.

Every time I lose my breakfast
someone tells me it is good,
a sign that I'll keep you.

BROTHERS ARE A BIG RESPONSIBILITY

I have a brother. I actually have two; one I got to keep, without any planning or effort on my part. The other I got to pick. Ed was four days old, small enough to lie on my Mom's arm, head nesting against her elbow, butt resting in the palm of her hand. We had gone to the adoption agency to collect him. I decided then that he was perfect, and that something so small needed my protection.

A few days later, someone told me that he wasn't completely ours yet. We would all have to go see the judge after a year, so that the judge could decide if we were a good family for him. I was furious. I was terrified. In dreams, a man I could not see told me that I couldn't keep Eddie. I never told anyone.

Talking about the nightmares would have made them real. I spent a lot of time awake, listening to Mom feed Eddie, every few hours, around the clock. I hovered in the background, making sure he was fine, until she sent me back to bed.

When we went to see the judge, dressed in church clothes, I felt sick. My head hurt; my curls were too tight, my ponytails pinched me. I balled up my fists, ready to defend my brother. I planned to throw myself at the judge and shout to my Mom to run out with Eddie.

The judge looked down at us, bunched together. I tried to look normal and happy and perfect. The hearing was a formality. All of the real testing and measuring had already been done. It didn't take long, and we walked out, holding

Ed, down the steps and back to our car. I wasn't sure what to do with all of the anger I had been saved up, or all of my fear. I felt it start to trickle away as we drove home.

CLOSE THE WINDOW, OPEN YOUR MIND

That one. You-simply-must-close-it-dearest-I-am-getting-a-terrible-chill. She always speaks in a high-pitched monotone, humming the words together. And she always asks me to close the window, which is always closed. I go through the next step of our ritual; I check all of the window latches in the dining room obsequiously, making sure that she can see me. None of them are open.

You-are-so-wonderful-to-take-care-of-a-dying-old-woman-darling. I-will-miss-you-when-I-go-to-heaven. I-will-smile-down-upon-you. I tell her that I will miss her too, and I will. We hold hands for a moment, while she waits for the carer to bring her plate. It is Tuesday, Meatloaf Day. She is soon humming, fork in hand, swirling chunks of meatloaf through ketchup, making patterns on her plate. Her humming is infectious; the dining room resonates with the *MMMmms* of 17 geriatric bees.

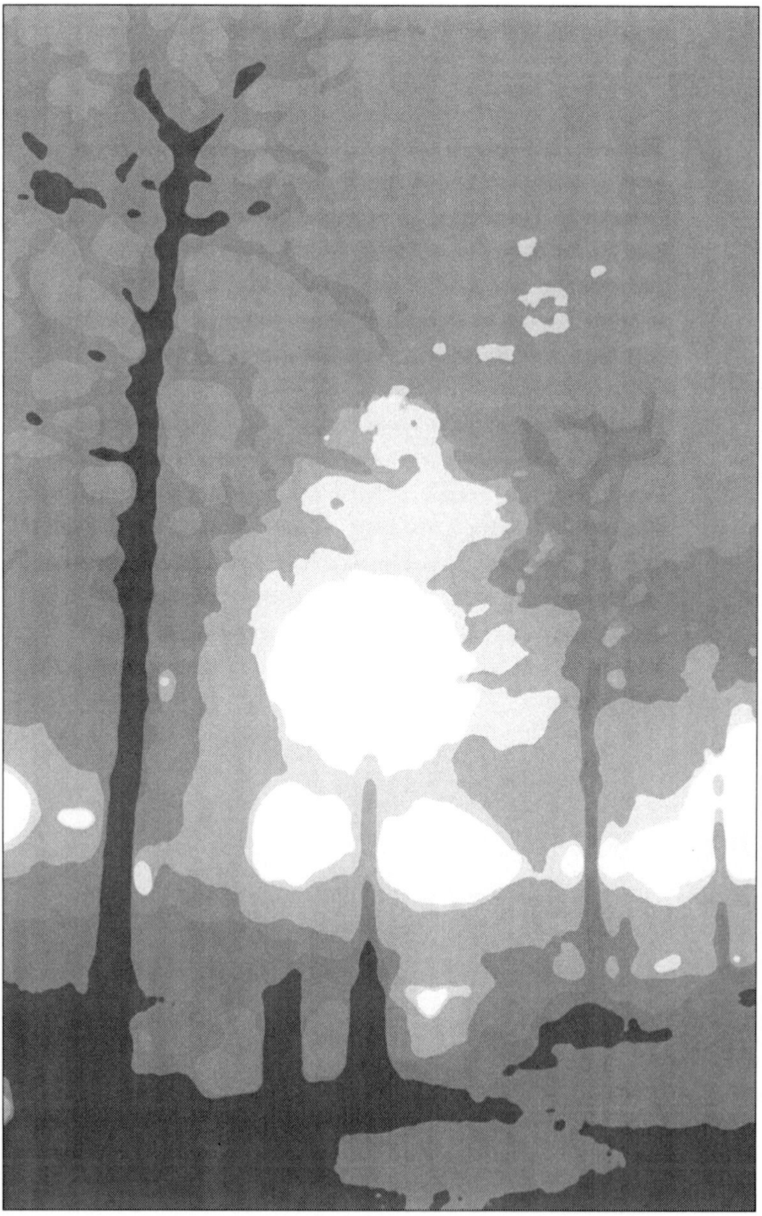

BLUE

Babies can be hard to keep,
harder still for untrue women—
something always goes wrong,
and their babies get lost.

Once you've got them, keeping babies
is the problem;
they don't have to be thrown down cliffs
or fed to their fathers to be
dead.

Dead is a whimper, an
exhalation in the quiet between
the dark and the light of morning.

Some babies fall asleep, don't wake up.
Some disappear so quickly
neighbours wonder if they imagined
swollen bellies and shuffling feet,
tiny squalls in the night.

Those are the babies that shouldn't have been.

We know.
They slip away, and
the world rights itself,
goes back to turning for the rest of us.

The lie is the true thing, though:
the cost of small, blue feet
that cannot be kept

the cost of sorry that cannot be heard
the weight of impotent cardigans
that will not be used:
too late for you, first one,
and your cold blue feet.

MY OLD BAG

I slouch
Forwards, backwards, sideways.
He is a squirming tangle of coathangers, string, cans, bones;
there is little room left for breath or breakfast.
Tucked up under my ribs
He bends them like bows,
Jabbing me with adversarial elbows.
I am a wineskin, overflowing with baby,
skin stretched taut.

I remember your handbags, vast
sacks of check books, grocery lists, lipsticks.
They didn't go anywhere without you.
You only set them down for babies, some borrowed,
passing the bags to me to look after.
They were full of things you carried for other people.

In wrinkled photos, you lean against a door frame,
A succession of babies on one hip.
Your face is haggard, chignon and lipstick perfect.
Is there time for another cigarette?

Later, the cigarettes and babies are gone.
Your face is pinched closed, skin worn hairless and smooth,
an old bag, stretched over your bones, life almost gone from
you.
I carry you in,
I carry your life in, bowed
under the weight of death and photos of babies.
I walk out, backpack in hand.
This is a bag I know;

it comforts me.
My life is in it.
There are no borrowed babies, no half-empty tubes of lipstick—

EVEN BUMBLEBEES STOP BUZZING EVENTUALLY

I saw my Bumblebee today; she was in bed, curled up in a ball, not humming. She didn't launch into her usual speech about drafts and windows. Her eyes were closed. I used to tease her, saying she was such a gossip that she must sleep with them open. The prospect of a sausage supper didn't get her buzzing. I asked why.

Her *gentleman-friend-with-terrible-manners* has died, and she doesn't want to eat without him. She asks me to take her wheelchair away. She doesn't need it *where-I-am-going-darling-and-I-will-smile-down-on-you-when-I-arrive*. I tucked in her blanket; she doesn't like to be cold. I wheeled the chair away, and told the GP that her heart was broken. Anyone ought to be able to diagnose that.

Woman's Work

DEAD LEG DREAMING

I can see snow. I can see my breath in front of my face. It is very early morning; the sun is almost up. We are cold: but I don't know who we are. I don't recognize anyone. I am in a cave. People stare. My knee itches. I try to scratch it; I feel bark. Smooth, peeling white bark, with black, thready veins running through it. I am wooden from the knee down.

The Dead Leg is a silver birch. I feel a certain relief at being able to name my Log accurately. I am still me, somehow, even in the chaos of dreams. Leaves sprouting in a ring around my kneecap wither and die almost immediately. I realize, abruptly, that everyone is waiting for me to pull the Dead Leg off, and put it in the embers of a fire. I pull, and it snaps off, leaves rustling. It lights quickly; it is sere, dead. The bark curls away, and flecks of it float in the updraft over the fire.

APPLE SNOW

I've been trying to type them up,
all these recipes,
asking questions,
keeping the cook in her alive.

The rest of her is dead.
The girl from the farm next door is gone,
my wife is gone, their mother is gone.

This one is for Apple Snow.

Take one large Bramley apple, a punnet of raspberries, or 3/4 pound of plums.
I don't know what 3/4 pound of plums feels like,
but she could always measure with her eyes, and know
when she had enough.

3 egg whites—no easy thing, separating the whites from the yolks, and she used to do it while she talked to me, or heard the weans' homework.

Whisk egg whites until stiff, add sugar to taste.
I cannae do it; I've tried,
they sag doon the bowl every time.
Maybe underbeaten, maybe over;
like science, and I was nae guid at that a'tall.

Stew fruit until cooked, add sugar to taste.
I can't even get her to taste the fruit.
She looks at it like it don't belong to her.
I cannae sieve they wee bits oot very well.

I ken that's mebbe why
she'll no' taste it: too bitty, too soor.

Fold into egg white.
Now it's all gone to hell in this bowl,
and she'll no' even laugh at me.
I can't read her either.

SATED

He hunts, blind, but not blind,
one eye open in mild animosity,
downy head furred in soft black.

He burrows, scenting the milk,
kneads with pink starfish paws,
mewls suspiciously.

Striking every warm and rounded muscle,
he surprises the crook of an arm,
latches on to an embarrassed knee.

Handed over, he clutches me,
knees pulled up, back arched,
all ecstatic greed:
grubbing, a mole, a boy.

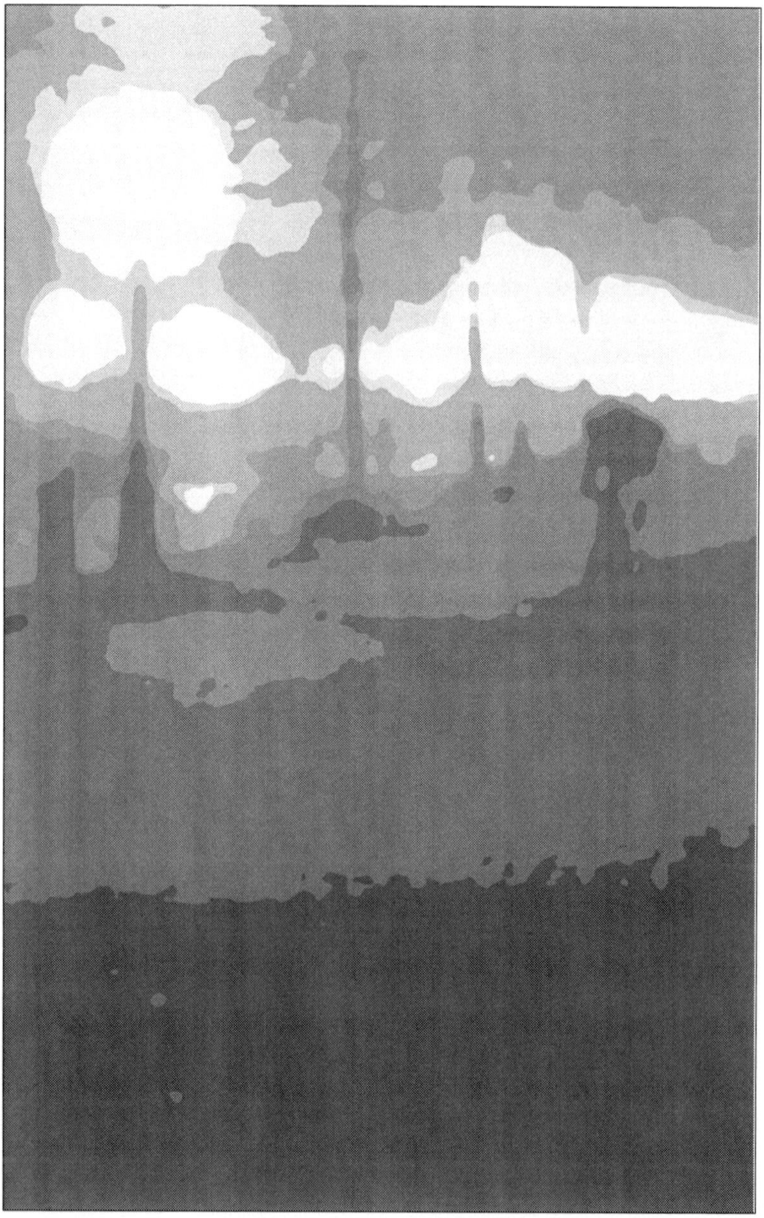

SEASONIN'

Every skillet needs a good seasonin'.

Best ones are cast iron, real heavy, a dirty grey colour, 'bout the size of a big dinner plate. You got to work on 'em until they blacken. Best way to do it is ta git out your can a' bacon grease.

You don't have one? Shame on you, girl!

No woman should evah be without her ol' coffee can a' grease. Y'all need one a' them old big ones. Ever' time you cook bacon, when the grease's cooled off, but it ain't turned that milky yella color, dump it in the can on top of the last batch. Save it up. Nothin' better for makin' beans have some taste, or crispin' up some fried eggs, or making you some hot water cornbread. Bacon grease is the answer to most cookin' questions. I cain't cook worth a durn without it.

Back to the seasonin'.

You need to wash the pan onc't. Pat it dry. Then you put it on the heat. Medium-high heat, and put you two or three big tablespoons a' that grease in it. Let the grease cook into it fo' a while. When it starts to smoke, turn it off. Move the pan to the back burner and forget about it fo' a while. All you gonna have to do is wipe it out with some paper towels.

Lord's sake, no!

Don't you wash it, Mary Frances, or you gonna wash all a'

that goodness out. No dish soap. Be plenty clean with a quick rinse under hot water and a wipe. Don't never soak it in water—you'll rust it, and you'll have to start all over with the seasonin'.

YOU ARE SUCH A WEE DARLING

The nurse is apologetic, tucking her hair behind her ears and fidgeting with a notepad. She isn't making a referral, not exactly. This worries her. Do I look that scary, I wonder? Or maybe just harassed?

> *She asked for you. Sorry…I had to call. I ken that youse are to'tly swamped, hen, but I couldnae let her leave w'y oot telling you goodbye.*

"I'm glad you called. She's really special to me. Doesn't matter how busy you think I might be," I can't explain just how much I appreciate having the chance to say goodbye. A catastrophic stroke usually steals the goodbye time—but not today.

Today, I get to hold a very wrinkly hand. I get to be human, to enjoy having someone *who remembers the dinosaurs* call me *wee darling*. I help her eat what may be her last bowl of strawberry ice cream. Statistics don't tell much of her story, or anyone's, really.

GOSPEL

Unequal will always call itself equal.

That's just how things are.

Since forever.

People talk about equal pay for equal work, but that don't never happen. No boss really means for it to happen.

Somebody's always the favourite.

That's human nature.

Honey, you are just gonna have to be better at everything you do than any boy is ever going to be.

Out of Memory

NATIVITY

Once I was beautiful;
blue dress, shoes shined.
On Christmas morning,
everyone can be new.

Blonde, sure of my body's perfection,
pupating, someone else
for 5 minutes.

My mother took a picture.
I have it now:
an aborted me
I would have liked to know.

KILLING WITH KINDNESS AND A COMPLIMENT

> *I'm sorry to be such a nuisance. I really don't know why I'm here.*

Pink Cardie is anxious. She knows she's seen me before, but isn't sure why, or when, or if we got along.

> *Just you ignore her, hen, like the rest'y us do. I'll no' listen to that tripe again today.*

Her frenemy, Pin Curls, is irritated—again—because *the feeble-minded auld yin* has a visitor and she doesn't.

> *I think I was here yesterday, but I'm simply not certain. Do I know you? Are you angry at me?*

Pink Cardie is very worried now; she doesn't like attracting Pin Curls' notice. I'm not angry at her, and I tell her so. I tell her she isn't a nuisance. I tell her, again, that I've come to see her, that I'm happy to be with her. She is in the Danger Zone, however, sitting right next to the sharpest tongue in the place.

> *Oh! My cardigan! I never noticed. I don't remember that hole being there. Look! The whole seam is out, all along the inside of my arm.*

Pink Cardie is frightened: her best jumper looks ruined, and she never even noticed.

> *She said the same thing yesterday. I noticed. I remember that big fookin' split*

> *all along her arm. I told her about it yesterday, too, hen, but she'll no' pay me any attention, not at all.*

Pin Curls frowns. I suggest that Pink Cardie might have forgotten. I point out that I forget things, and I don't even have dementia.

> *Yet.*

Pin Curls mutters, darkly, glowering, chins and rollers bobbing in agitation.

> *Do you think I've an unfortunate manner, lassie? Are youse tellin' me I wasnae polite tae her?*

"I am. I enjoy coming in and talking to you, but there's no reason for you to humiliate her. She forgot. We all forget things. She wears the cardigan a lot because it is her favorite." Pin Curls decides to make peace.

> *Aye, right, I suppose so, hen, and no hard feelins, as it is a lovely colour on you, and fair shows off them red splodges of blush ye've put on yer cheeks.*

RIDING THE DEMENTIA EXPRESS

She carries it against her chest, holding it just as I am holding my notebook and diary. I have scurried through sleet, across a parking lot, protecting my things from the wet.

She waits, holding the picture of the person she used to be: a talisman, to ward off disaster. But her disaster has already happened: she has dementia, *unspecified, no known etiology.* Dementia is relentlessly efficient, an express train to madness. She has been dumped at the terminus, and, somehow, she knows that the service only runs in one direction.

She keeps pointing to the people in the picture. Her husband first, then her children. I tell her their names. She points to herself; "that's you," I say. "There you are." She taps her photograph self, then stabs her physical self in the forehead with a dirty index finger. *Bye bye? Bye Bye?* She asks me again, and again, and I don't know if this means she wants me to leave, wants me to stay, wants to leave herself and never come back.

Tap. Tap. TAP!! A rising crescendo of despair. I am afraid the glass will break, but she does. She cries, and rocks, grieving for the woman in the photograph. I hold her hand as I tell her who she is, saying her name over and over, until she closes her eyes.

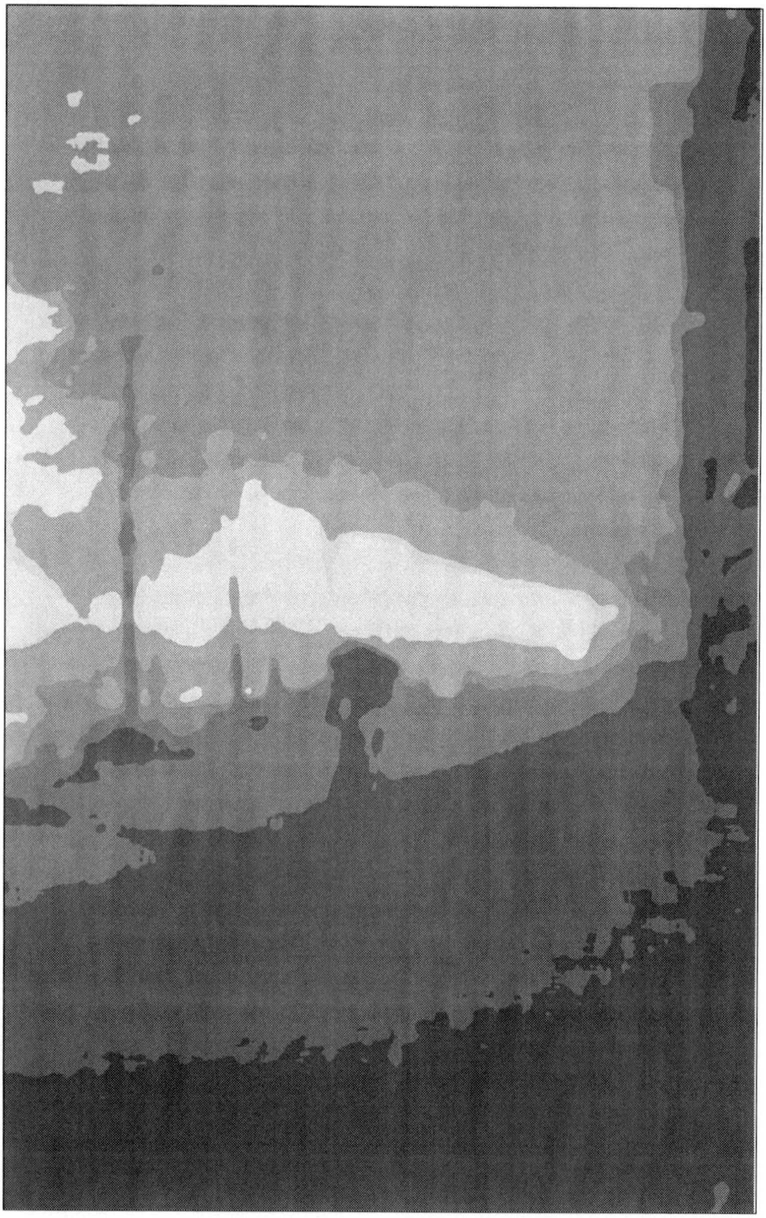

PURPLE

You look lovely.
That colour really suits you!
Green. Green is beautiful.

> *Have a good look.*
> *It is actually purple.*

Ach, stupid me, So it is.
Purple is a lovely shade of green.

BYE BYE BABY

Her anxiety is immense, and I don't know what to do about it. Does she want me to stay? Does she want me to go? Is *bye bye baby* just my name now? I tell her that I will be back in a few days. She is thinner now; I hold her hands, all knuckles and bones, and see the blue veins, the chewed fingernails, fluttering. She is still here, but for how much longer?

STILL TICKING

She is agitated today; even lying down, too weak to stand, she is in constant, frenzied movement. Her eyes flick from my face to her picture, from her photographed face back to my face. She points, and waits for me to say my name, and then her name, over and over. She holds my hand and rocks back and forth.

WEBBED

A corpulent spider
presides over the ruins of herself,
Tangled
In her cotton-white sheets and hair,
Barking orders,
Scanning with opal-lensed eyes.

Nurses scuttle.
She throws forks, soup,
hissing through 7 teeth,
demanding her daughters, her babies:
Where have you took them! Bitches!

FAMILY SECRETS

All families have at least one. Shameful ones, dark ones, sad ones. 'Premature' babies born before they should have been; babies who looked like family friends, rather than their fathers; women who did anything to keep food on the table, when men couldn't or wouldn't work. Most of these secrets are harboured by women; they respect and fear them enough not to misplace or forget the secrets. They love the rest of us enough not to tell the secrets publicly.

I know what happens to families when the secret-keeping mothers and grandmothers die or, dementing, forget and are themselves lost. Families unravel, as if the secret no one knew or talked about was the thing that kept the family together. I hear secret things, things no one else has ever heard, and try to keep the secrets safe, because they might be all that my patients have left of who they were or were not allowed to be.

CLOCK

My head is a clock
My pulse, loud....tock.
Time crawls across my face—
stretching skin, wrinkles race.

Love Is

MAKING THE BED

I make our bed this morning, pulling off the old sheet—flick.
Cotton crumples to the floor behind me; I don't look back.
Years of long practice: I know where it will land.

I shake the duvet cover, holding with both hands, and flick.
I turn it inside out: snap.
I wear the cover, winged arms wide, bending to grab corners
as hidden feathers slide and bunch under polyester skin.

I flick, pulling my elbows in, and step back from the bed
as the duvet swings and settles,
hummocked turf
over rocks and hills.
I smooth it, claiming us.
My hands are certain of the outcome.
I never iron sheets, because your mother would have.

I made our bed. I'll lie in it.
Poised between yes and no,
stay and go,
I'll lie in it.

Ambivalence is the terrain of love.
Beneath accumulated wrongs, across time,
I love you. I know this, as my hands know the sheets.

But I hesitate:
I might drop us.
I don't know where we will land.
I cannot always remake us, smooth us back together.
I can't wash us, dry us, flick us inside out, and right us again.

OPPOSITE OF

Don't ever let anyone call you Mrs.
I don't.
No Missus was ever decadent:
always about laundry, diapers, dusting,
never passion or glamour,
never accused of appearing *in flagrante delicto*,
never papped, fox-fur clad, strolling to her limo.

COMPASS

You opened the door into silence, closed the curtains;
and there were no families, no stars.

I did not know you: no compass made
my way plain, no words my meanings clear.
All that had gone before meant nothing.

Sussura of sheets, singing static as
blankets drifted to the floor,
and with them all reserve—

We bathed in love, a sea of it,
our world was one bed wide.

Discarded clothes, an archipelago;
shoes scattered leeward.

Half-lidded, I watched the world
shrink further, winking out.

I could not look at you, or speak,
but mapped you with my hands.

NOT HERE

You are
half-way down the stairs,
closer to the front door & away
than to me in our
lonely kitchen.

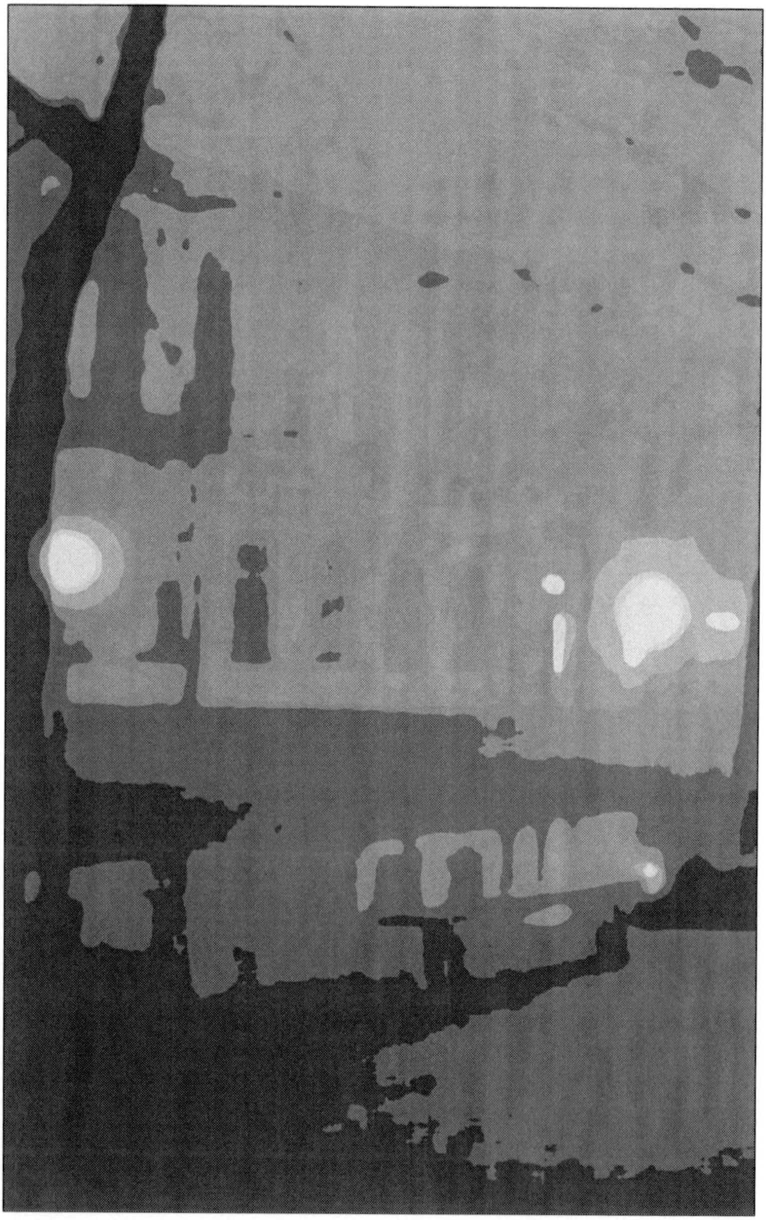

ALLIES AND ENEMIES

> *They just cannae stand each ither, hen. It's f'y auld reasons, y'ken, auld ones. The one lived doon th' street f'y the other for 40, 50 year.*

The nursing assistant eyes them warily.

> *They may not be far enough apart, hen. Can you help me move this lady over there?*

Glasses and Necklaces don't even open their eyes any more. But they can tell when "she" comes into the dining room, and God help anyone foolish enough to let them sit near each other.

> *Bit of blethering…blethering,*

Necklace announces, eyes squeezed shut.

> *Where'd ya go w'y that? Ya sit and sleep, thats a' ye dae. What do youse ken aboot anythin'? Sleepin' yer time away a' th' day, screamin' a'th' night?*

> *I like a cigar, now and then.*

Necklace can afford to be polite; she's been victorious for decades.

> *I would nivver hae a cigarette; they smell mingin' tae me, y'ken. My Dad put a bit of*

> *that pepper in his thingummy pipe and I smoked it when I was wee.*

> *That's nothin' tae dae w'onythin'; there youse go agin. Wheesht. That lassie doesnae care aboot yer smokin' history.*

Glasses is right; it is nothing to do with me, neither here nor there.

> *She'll damn well care if I skelp youse, and knock youse doon they stairs.*

Necklace takes her gloves off.

> *Smokin' and talking aboot it all daiy lang can get youse kilt. Dinnae tell me aboot skelpin' an' tha' or I'm just gonnae do f'y ye.*

Bickering quickly flares into nuclear war. Mince, tatties, and insults fly. Even when they don't know who they are any more, they can still remember the man they both loved, who married someone else. He married Wig, and she is the real winner here, 50 years later.

PARASITE

I can hear her: noisy, this one.
She's unpacked her bags,
made herself at home between us.
Our garden isn't ours any more.

Ugly, now she's dropped her mask,
furious maggot-white face
peering out between your words.

She fills all of the pauses, all of the gaps,
rearranges, orchestrating arguments.
I retreat, you accuse, I ask, you deny: she feeds.

She plays house in your head,
rooting around, shoving things out of the way,
rump firmly jammed against 'love' as she kicks at 'you'
furiously, and soon enough, it gets knocked out of the way;
you forget the 'you,' the 'me,' that was there.

WAVE THE WHITE DISHTOWEL

No subtle signal
is ever good enough.
Everything has to be written large,
embarrassingly large,
to make sense to you.

Head in an oven?
Yes.
Perfect.
Now you know that I am hurt.

An explanation,
a request,
cutting off an arm or leg,
would never be enough.

THE DAMN THING WON'T FIT

Nothing is right, today, hen. I cannae get this damn thing on, and I dinnae ken what ya'd call the shitty thing. I feel like half a woman, hen, and that's the truth. I don't want anyone to see me. I wish I could just destroy myself!

Wig wants to look perfect. Her husband is coming to visit, and she can't get her wig on straight. I guess love doesn't get any easier when *yer auld, hen, and ye dinnae ken why they stay w'you.*

I take her wig off. She is shinily bald. My face stretches and curves around her scalp, like the glass reflecting ball in the garden. I turn the wig around, plop it back on her head, and shoogle it into place. "It was just on back to front. That's the wig sorted. Need a bit of lippy?" Wig relaxes and winks.

PATIENCE

Bore me with details.
Tell me all about your rotten childhood,
aborted dreams,
the heartless boss who never understands.

Your hands wring out well-rehearsed grievances.
The word-flood slows.
I watch your mouth,
waiting—
how best to distract you?
Bodies have their own efficient vernacular.

Endings

LAST

No one here but me, you know.
I'm all that's left.
My sisters were 101 and 104 when they died—
I had them too long, but I still miss them.
My husband is dead.
My son too.
All of my friends are gone.
Just me left; I've lived too long.

SACKING THE OLD BAG

They swooped down,
after you died, almost like
troops scavenging after the fall of some citadel or other,
in a place I couldn't remember.

I would have left the blouses, the dresses,
silk and denim rustling in their plastic
dry cleaner's chrysalids,
always, imagining
I could hear the coathangers scraping down the rail as you
hemmed and hawed.

They didn't want anything to go to waste,
they said,
so they laid waste
to your closet and drawers. I'm sure
vultures have their reasons
for leaving nothing.

> *We'll sort her things so you don't have to do it.*

> *None of these things will fit you.*

> *This dress is too good to give away
> to some homeless person: besides,
> I have always loved it.*

Justifications
for ransacking you,
because
you were your clothes.

Your clothes still smelled of
you
Even though you weren't inside of them,
weren't, in fact,
you
any more.

Anywhere.

BATTERY GRANNIES

The tour starts here. This is the Activity Room.
I would ask that you don't open any doors, or go anywhere
without a member of staff. Please stay on the green carpet.

We want the best for our residents.
We offer everything they need—positive freedom, freedom:
*from hunger and thirst; from discomfort; from pain; injury or
disease; to express normal behaviour; from fear and distress.*

Don't feed them.
This isn't a petting zoo.

Some of them are still very slender, but
they come to us in terrible shape,
most of them, so we fatten them up.
No one ever wants a scrawny one, but we stock
all shapes, makes, and models.

We feed them regularly.
Food is supplied in place.
They quickly learn to eat
things
they don't recognize, if
they get hungry enough,
though the weaker ones get pushed aside. Occasionally.
Which
leads to other problems, which then require
somewhat
harsher remedies:
*The de-beaking of chickens is deprecated, but it is recognized
that it is a method of last resort, seen as better than allowing*

vicious fighting and ultimately cannibalism.

Their legs don't always work, unfortunately, but
this will not affect your statutory rights.
*Because they cannot move easily, the chickens are not able to
adjust their environment to avoid heat, cold or dirt as they
would in natural conditions.*

Some have strange *hock burns*; do-gooders accuse us of
leaving occupants lying in their own shit,
but we just can't train them to stand.
We feed them, but then
they cannot support their increased body weight.
First too weak, then too fat. A conundrum.

All are functional, to some extent. They
learn to mimic natural behaviour.
We train them not to chirp
or squeak,
and never let them pray.

Research suggests that they benefit from participating
in meaningful activity:
we encourage bingo and crochet.
*Physical restraints are used to control movement or actions
regarded as undesirable.*

The telly works for some of them.
they don't know what they're missing.
Reception's not an issue;
they're content with static and with hissing.

Piled here,
they take up very little space.
Confinement at high stocking density is one part a systematic

effort to produce the highest output at the lowest cost.
We do our best for the shareholders and customers.
There's a warehoused granny for everyone.

Borrowed material indicated in italics; see
source texts in addendum.

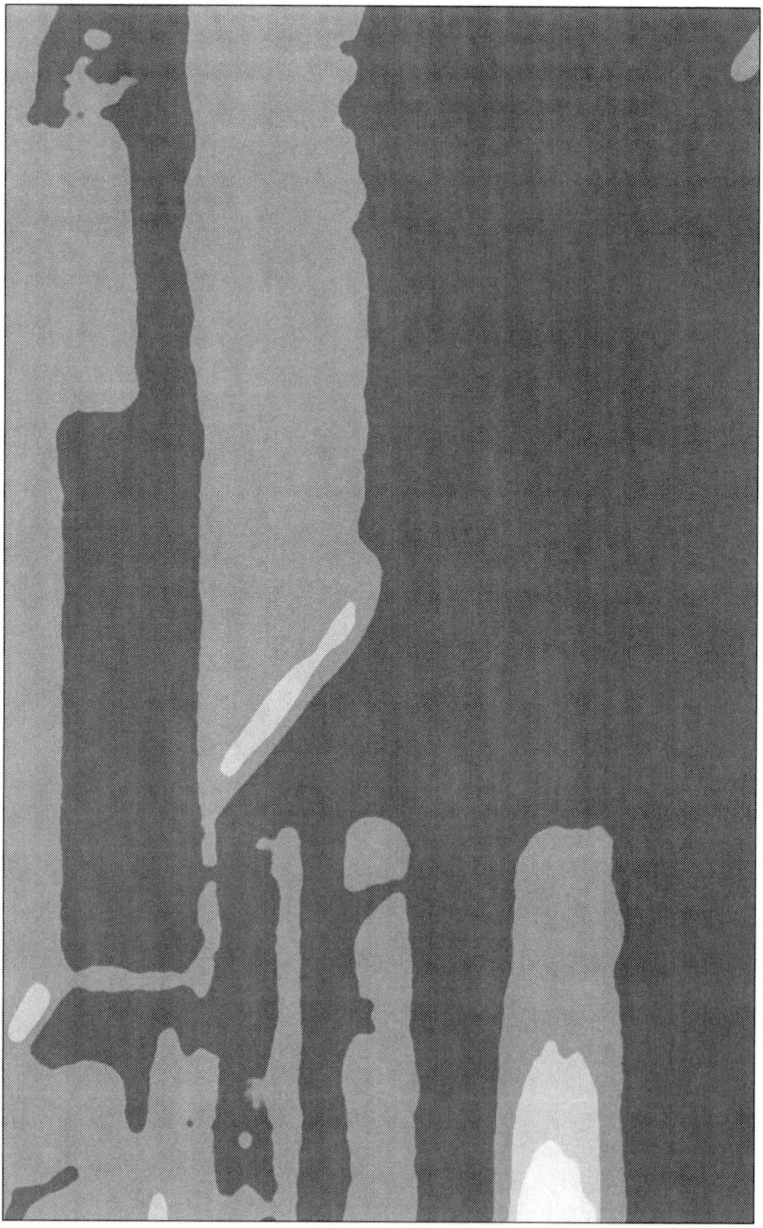

LORDY, HALLELUJAH, AND BROWNKAYDIS

I got a list a' thangs, Mary Fances, and most of 'em are bad. Brownkaydis, hardery of the artery, emphysema, and LORD! Don't even get me started on the problems at the rear end from all the damn medicine.

At least I haven't gone senile yet. I don't have dementia, and I ain't losing my house or my mind. Not just yet, anyways. You'd tell me if I wasn't making no sense no more, Mary Frances. I know you would.

At least with my aneurism, ain't nobody gonna be able to do nothin' crazy like bringing me back as a vegetable. Lordy! I'd hate that. Way things are with my aneurism, I'm just gonna go, it'll be fast, and I won't be in no pain or be any kinda bother to nobody. I just don't want nobody to find me dead, cause that might upset them. I wisht it could just happen while I'm driving, and I would hit a concrete overpass or something, then I'd know nobody could keep me here. Everyone I know is dead, seems like, and I've seen all I wanna see. Don't envy you, bringing up children nowadays. Drugs and designer clothes- Lordy! Just wouldn't know what to do with them once they was out of size 6x. They don't wanna be bothered by an ol' woman after that.

MORE BROKEN

She has lost her 'hallelujah'. She croons *ah-oo, a-le-oo; ah-oo; a-le-lo*o, as soon as she sees me. Her sadness, palpable, washes over and sticks to me. *Ah-oo? Ah-le-loo?*, she insists, as I try to get her to drink. She takes a few sips, and coughs, weakly, before chanting *ah-oo, a-le-loo* again. She isn't swallowing any more; she can't; the neurologic program is gone, another thing she has lost. She will not sleep. There is nothing I can do but hold her hand, so I do that. She cries a little, and the insistent *ah-oo? a-le-loo?* subsides. Her sadness ebbs; it has a rhythm I don't understand, rising and falling, tidal as breath. She is slipping away, trickling away from herself and from me. I let go of her hand. As I close the door, she says *Bye bye, baby.*

I say "Hallelujah. Goodbye." And I mean it.

TODAY THERE ARE NO MORE HALLELUJAHS

She died in her sleep, sitting in a chair. She was gone, slipping away quietly between one breath and the next, with no one to catch her or keep her here. Her photograph fell to the ground beside her. We have all been waiting, as she has been. It is very quiet today; all of the residents are subdued, even the ones whom the nurses assume, wrongly, don't understand anything. They can read us, they can read me; they touch me, and each other, as they shuffle past on zimmers, looping around the hallways and past the elevator. No more *hallelujah*, no more *bye bye, baby,* no more trying to explain dementia to someone who knows she can't understand.

I say 'bye, bye, baby,' as I drive away,
and I mean it.

WE SWIM OUT

We swim out
but always seek
the return to waters we know,
sailors more than most:
an honest reunion,
Death in saltwater.

We are water,
chaff blown loose without,
Lethe, Nile, one source
in our dreams:
reflections
ripple outward, then still.

Source texts

The following source texts are used in Battery Grannies:

"The 90-plus age group, or the 'oldest old,' is the fastest growing segment of the population, according to the U.S. Census. While there are currently nearly 2 million nonagenarians in the U.S. alone, that number is projected to increase to 10 to 12 million by the middle of the century, raising concerns that the current health care system may not be able to accommodate this population." *University of California - Irvine. "Women Over 90 More Likely To Have Dementia Than Men." ScienceDaily, 5 Jul. 2008. Web. Sep 2011*

"Confinement at high stocking density is one part of a systematic effort to produce the highest output at the lowest cost" "Factory farms hold large numbers of animals, typically cows, pigs, turkeys, or chickens, often indoors, typically at high densities. The aim of the operation is to produce as much meat, eggs, or milk at the lowest possible cost. Food is supplied in place, and a wide variety of artificial methods are employed to maintain animal health and improve production, such as the use of antimicrobial agents, vitamin supplements, and growth hormones. Physical restraints are used to control movement or actions regarded as undesirable. Breeding programs are used to produce animals more suited to the confined conditions and able to provide a consistent food product." Wikipedia contributors. "Intensive animal farming." *Wikipedia, The Free Encyclopedia, 18 Dec. 2013. Web. Sep 2011*

"For example, in the UK, de-beaking of chickens is deprecated, but it is recognized that it is a method of last resort, seen as better than allowing vicious fighting and ultimately cannibalism." "In the UK, the Farm Animal Welfare Council was set up by the government to act as an independent advisor on animal welfare in 1979 and expresses its policy as five freedoms: from hunger & thirst; from discomfort; from pain, injury or disease; to express normal behavior; from fear and distress." "In intensive broiler sheds, the air can become highly polluted with ammonia from the droppings. This can damage the chickens' eyes and respiratory systems and can cause painful burns on their legs (called hock burns) and feet. Chickens bred for fast growth have a high rate of leg deformities. Because they cannot move easily, the chickens are not able to adjust their environment to avoid heat, cold or dirt as they would in natural conditions. The added weight and overcrowding also puts a strain on their hearts and lungs. In the U.K., up to 19 million chickens die in their sheds from heart failure each year." Wikipedia contributors. "Poultry farming." *Wikipedia, The Free Encyclopedia, 25 Dec. 2013. Web. Sep 2011*